The BASIL BR
Song Book

ILLUSTRATED BY

BABETTE COLE

WISE PUBLICATIONS

Illustrations by Babette Cole
Music selected by Frank Johnson
Production supervised by Robert Sampson

Exclusive distributors:
Music Sales Limited,
78 Newman Street,
London W1P 3LA,
England.

Music Sales Pty. Limited,
27 Clarendon Street,
Artarmon,
Sydney, NSW 2064,
Australia.

Printed by Lowe & Brydone Ltd., Thetford, England.

Contents

Cockles and Mussels

1. In Dub-lin's fair ci-ty, where girls are so pret-ty, I first set my eyes on sweet Mol-ly Ma-lone, As she wheel'd her wheel-bar-row through streets broad and nar-row, Cry-ing, 'Cock-les and Mus-sels! A-live, a-live oh!
2. She was a fish mon-ger, but sure t'was no won-der, For so were her fa-ther and Moth-er be-fore And they each wheel'd their bar-row through streets broad and nar-row, Cry-ing, 'Cock-les and Mus-sels! A-live, a-live oh!
Chorus
A-live, a-live, oh! A-live, a-live oh!' Cry-ing, 'Cock-les and Mus-sels, a-live, a-live oh!'
D.C.

3. She died of a fever, and no one could save her,
And that was the end of sweet Molly Malone;
Her ghost wheels her barrow
through streets broad and narrow,
Crying, 'Cockles and mussels, alive, alive oh!
Alive, alive oh! etc.

M. MALONE
COCKLES & MUSSELS

Ding Dong Bell

Ding dong bell! Pus - sy's in the well! Who put her in?
Lit - tle Tom - my Green. Who pulled her out? Lit - tle Tom - my Stout. What a
naugh - ty boy was that To drown poor pus - sy cat, Who
ne'er did a - ny harm, But killed all the mice in his
fa - ther's barn.

English Country Garden

1. How ma - ny gen - tle flow - ers grow in an Eng - lish Coun - try Gar - den. I'll tell you now of some I know and those I miss, I hope you'll par - don. gen - tle lu - pin and tall hol - ly hocks, Ros - es Daf - fo - dils, hearts sea - son flocks, Mea - dow sweet and lil - ies stocks fox - gloves snow - drops, For - get - me - nots, In an
2. How ma - ny in - sects find their home in an Eng - lish Coun - try Gar - den. I'll tell you now of some I know and those I miss, I hope you'll par - don. But - ter - flies sway in the mild gen - tle breeze, There are Dra - gon - flies moths and bees, Spi - ders fall - ing from the trees hedge - hogs that roam, And lit - tle gnomes, In an
p
mp
mf

1 - 2
Eng - lish Coun - try Gar - den.
Eng - lish Coun - try p Gar - den.
3
ritard.

3. How many song birds make their nests
In an English Country Garden.
I'll tell you now of some I know
And those I miss, I hope you'll pardon.
Babelling coo cooing doves,
Robins and the warbling thrush,
Bluebird, lark, finch and nightingale,
We all smile in the spring
When the birds all start to sing,
In an English Country Garden.

Food, Glorious Food

1. Food, Glo - ri - ous Food! Hot saus - age and mus - tard! While we're in the
2. Food, Glo - ri - ous Food! Don't care what it looks like, Burned, un - der - done
mood, Cold jel - ly and cus - tard! Pease pud - ding and sav - e - loys,
crude, Don't care what the cooks like, Just think - ing of grow - ing fat,
"What next?" is the ques - tion. Rich gen - tle - men have it, boys, in - dye -
Our sen - ses are reel - ing, One mo - ment of know - ing that full up
- ges - tion! Food, Glo - ri - ous Food! We're an - xious to try it,
feel - ing! Food, Glo - ri - ous Food! What would - n't we give for.
Three ban - quets a day, Our fa - vour - ite di - et!
That ex - tra bit more. That's all we live for,
Just pic - ture a great big steak, fried, roast - ed or stewed. Oh,
Why should we be fat - ed to do noth - ing but brood. Oh,

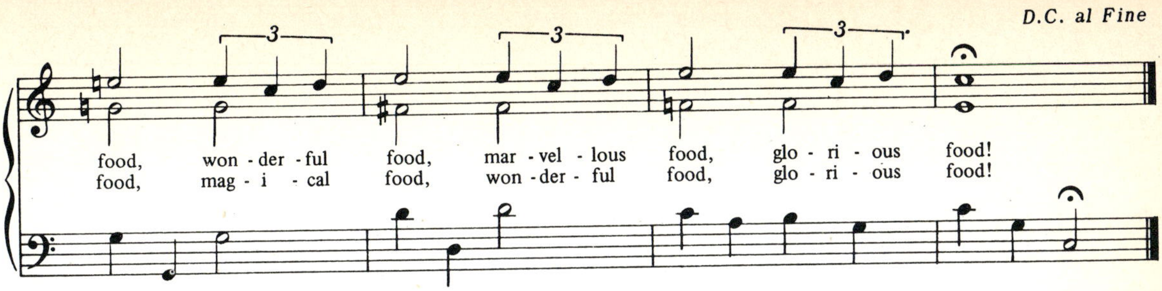
D.C. al Fine
3
food, won - der - ful food, mar - vel - lous food, glo - ri - ous food!
food, mag - i - cal food, won - der - ful food, glo - ri - ous food!

Going To The Zoo

Allegro
Dad - dy's tak - ing us to the zoo to - mor - row, zoo to - mor - row,
See the el - e - phant with the long trunk swing-ing Great big ears and
zoo to - mor - row, Dad - dy's tak - ing us to the zoo to - mor - row,
long trunk swing-ing Sniff - in' up pea-nuts with the long trunk swing- in'
Chorus
we can stay all day. We're go - ing to the zoo, zoo,
we can stay all day.
zoo, how a - bout you, you, you? You can come
too, too, too; we're go - ing to the zoo, zoo, zoo.
D.C.

3. See all the monkeys scritch, scritch scratchin'
Jumpin' all around and scritch, scritch, scratchin',
Hangin' by their long tails scritch, scritch, scratchin',
We can stay all day.

(Chorus)

4. Big black bear all huff huff a-puffin'
Coat's too heavy, he's huff huff a-puffin',
Don't get too near the huff huff a-puffin',
Or you won't stay all day.

(Chorus)

5. Seals in the pool all honk, honk, honkin',
Catchin' fish and honk, honk, honkin',
Little seals honk, honk, honkin', (high pitched voice)
We can stay all day.

(Chorus)

Slower Tempo

6. We stayed all day and I'm gettin' sleepy,
Sittin' in the car gettin' sleep, sleep, sleepy,
Home already and I'm sleep, sleep, sleepy,
We have stayed all day.

(Chorus)

Up Tempo

7. Mamma's taking us to the zoo tomorrow, zoo tomorrow,
Zoo tomorrow,
Momma's taking us to the zoo tomorrow;
We can stay all day.

(Chorus)

We've been to the zoo, zoo, zoo,
So have you you you
You came too, too, too;
We've been to the zoo, zoo, zoo.

(Chorus)

I'd Like To Teach The World To Sing

Moderately
mf
I'd like to build the world a home_ and fur - nish it with love_ Grow
ap - ple trees and hon - ey bees_ and snow-white tur - tle doves._ I'd
like to teach the world to sing_ in per - fect har - mo - ny_ I'd
like to see the world for once_ all stand - ing hand in hand,_ And
1
like to hold it in my arms_ and keep it com - pa - ny_ I'd
hear them ech - o
2
Fine
through the hills_ for peace through-out the land._ That's the song I hear,

let the world sing to - day. A song of peace that ech-oes on and
nev - er goes a - way. Put your hand in my hand, Let's be -gin to -
D.S. al Fine
day. Put your hand in my hand, Help me find the way. I'd

I Taut I Taw A Puddy-Tat

Brightly
Verse
1. There is a lit - tle ti - ny bird, his name is "Twee - ty Pie!" He lives in - side a bird - cage, a - hang - ing 'way up high. He likes to sit up - on his perch, so hap - py and so gay, But when a cat comes af - ter him you'll al - ways hear him cry.
2. There is a great big bad old cat, Syl - ves - ter is his name, He on - ly has one aim in life and that is ve - ry plain He dreams of catch - ing Twee - ty Pie, and eat - ing him one day. But just as he gets close e - nough Twee - ty gets a - way.

Chorus

I taut I taw a pud - dy tat a creep - in' up on
me. I did, I taw a pud - dy tat as plain as he could be.
D. C.

3. Tweety sometimes takes a walk and goes outside his cage,
But gets back before the cat and throws him in a rage.
Sylvester'd love to eat that bird if he could just get near,
But ev'ry time that he comes by, this is all he'll hear, (Chorus)

4. And when he sings that little song, his mistress knows he's home,
She grabs her broom and brings it down upon Sylvester's dome.
So there's no need of worrying, he lives just like a king,
And Puddy Tats can't hurt that bird as long as he can sing, (Chorus)

Lavender's Blue

1. Lav - en - der's blue, dil - ly, dil - ly, Lav - en - der's green,
2. Call up your men, dil - ly, dil - ly, Set them to work,
When I am King, dil - ly, dil - ly, You shall be queen.
Some to the plough dil - ly, dil - ly, Some to the cart.

3. Some to make hay, dilly, dilly,
   Some to cut corn,
   While you and I, dilly, dilly,
   Keep ourselves warm.

4. Lavender's green, dilly, dilly,
   Lavender's blue,
   If you love me, dilly, dilly,
   I will love you.

19
G. KIER
Tyler Hill
06

Where And Oh Where Has My Little Dog Dog Gone?

Oh where and oh where is my lit - tle dog
gone? Oh where and oh where can he be?
With his ears cut short, and his tail cut
long, Oh where, oh where is he?

The Little White Duck

Chorus
1. There's a lit - tle white duck sit - ting in the wat - er A
lit - tle green frog swim - ming in the wat - er A
lit - tle white duck Do - ing what he ought - er, He took a bite of a
lit - tle green frog Do - ing what he ought - er, He jumped right off of a
lil - ly pad Flapped his wings and he
lil - ly pad That the lit - tle duck bit and he
said, "I'm glad I'm a lit - tle white duck sit - ting in the wat - er"
said, "I'm glad I'm a lit - tle green frog swim - ming in the wat - er"

1,2,3,4
5
quack, quack, quack. 2. There's a
glumph, glumph, glumph.

3. (There's a) Little black bug floating in the water
A little black bug doing what he oughter,
He tickled the frog on the lily pad
That the little duck bit and he said,
"I'm glad I'm a little black bug floating on the water"
chirp, chirp, chirp. 4. (There's a)

4. Little red snake lying in the water
Little red snake doing what he oughter,
He frightened the duck and the frog so bad
Hit the little bug and he said,
"I'm glad I'm a little red snake lying in the water"
sss, sss, sss. 5. (Now there's)

5. Nobody left sitting in the water
Nobody left doing what he oughter,
There's nothing left but the lily pad
It's sad that there's nobody left
Boo, hoo, hoo.

Oh Dear What Can The Matter Be?

Quickly
1. Oh dear! what can the mat-ter be? Dear, dear! What can the mat-ter be?
Oh dear! What can the mat - ter be? John-ny's so long at the Fair. He
He
(End here)
pro-mised he'd buy me a fair ring to please me, And then for a kiss Oh! he vowed he would tease me; He
pro-mised he'd bring me a bask-et of pos - ies, A gar-land of lil - ies, a gar - land of ro - ses A
pro - mised he'd bring me a bunch of blue rib - bons To tie up my bon - ny brown hair.
lit - tle straw hat, to set off the blue rib - bons That tie up my bon - ny brown hair.
(Go back to beginning)

Yellow Submarine

Moderato
1. In the town where I was born lived a man who sailed to
sailed on to the sun, till we found the sea of
sea And he told us of his life in the land of sub-ma-
green; And we lived be-neath the waves, in our yel-low sub-ma-
1,3
rines. 2. So we
2,4
rine.
Chorus
We all live in a Yel-low sub-ma-rine,
Yel-low sub-ma-rine,
1 (3 & repeat Chorus to fade)
Yel-low sub-ma-rine.
2
Yel-low sub-ma-rine. 3. And our
D.S. & finally repeat Chorus as marked

3. And our friends are all aboard, many more of them live next door;
And the band begins to play, in our Yellow Submarine.

4. As we live a life of ease, ev'ry one of us has all we need;
Sky of blue and sea of green, in our Yellow Submarine....... *To Chorus & repeat ad lib to fade.*

Puff (The Magic Dragon)

Verse
1. Puff the mag - ic drag - on lived by the sea And
(To) ge - ther they would tra - vel on a boat with bill - owed sail
frol - icked in the au - tumn mist in a land called Ho - nah
Jack - ie kept a look - out perched on Puff's gi - gan - tic
Lee, Lit - tle Jack - ie Pa - per
tail Nob - le Kings and prin - ces would
loved that ras - cal Puff And
bow when e'er they came

brought him strings and sealing wax and other fancy stuff. Oh!
Pirate ships would low'r their flag when Puff roared out his name Oh!
Refrain
Puff, the magic dragon lived by the sea And
frolicked in the autumn mist in a land called Honah Lee,
Puff the magic dragon lived by the sea And
D.C. al Fine
frolicked in the autumn mist in a land called Honah Lee. 2. To-

3. A dragon lives for ever but not so little boys
Painted wings and giant rings make way for other toys.
One grey night it happened Jackie Paper came no more
And Puff the mighty dragon he ceased his fearless roar.

(Refrain)

4. His head was bent in sorrow, green scales fell like rain,
Puff no longer went to play along the cherry lane.
Without his life long friend Puff could not be brave
So Puff the mighty dragon sadly slipped into his cave.

(Refrain)

Tie A Yellow Ribbon Round The Ole Oak Tree

Brightly
Verse
mf
1. I'm com - ing home I've done my time, Now I've got to know what is and is - n't mine If you re-ceived my let-ter tel - lin' you I'd soon be free Then you'll know just what to do If you still want me? If you still want me?
2. Bus dri - ver please look for me, 'Cause I could-n't bear to see what I might see I'm real - ly still in pri - son and my love she holds the key A sim - ple yel - low rib - bon's what I need to set me free. I wrote and told her please. Well
Refrain
tie a yel - low rib - bon round the ole oak tree it's been three long

years do ya still want me? If I don't see a rib-bon _ 'round the
ole oak tree. _ I'll stay on the bus, For - get a - bout us, put the blame on
me, If I don't see a yel-low rib-bon 'round the ole oak tree. _
1
2
tree. _
ritard...
Slow and Rubato
Now the whole damn bus is cheer-ing and I can't believe I see _ A
Tempo I
hun-dred yel-low ribbons 'round the ole, ole oak tree. _
3

When I'm Sixty-four Four

Medium bounce

1. When I get old - er los -ing my hair_ man- y years from now._
2. I could be han - dy mending a fuse_ when your lights have gone._
Will you still be sending me a Val - en - tine,_ birth-day greet-ings, bot-tle of wine?_
You can knit a sweater by the fire - side,_ Sun-day morn-ings go for a ride._
If I'd been out_ till quarter to three_ would you lock_ the door?_
Do-ing the gar - den, dig-ging the weeds_ who could ask_ for more?_
Will you still need_ me, will you still feed_ me, when I'm six - ty four?_
Will you still need_ me, will you still feed_ me, when I'm six - ty four?_

3. Send me a postcard drop me a line
Stating point of view
Indicate precisely what you mean to say,
Yours sincerely wasting away.
Give me an answer, fill in a form
Mine for ever more.
Will you still need me,
will you still feed me,
When I'm sixty four?

D.C. al Fine

This Old Man

1. This old man, he played one, He played nick-nack on my drum:
2. This old man, he played two, He played nick-nack on my shoe
Nick-nack, pad-dy whack, give a dog a bone, This old man came roll-ing home.
Nick-nack, pad-dy whack, give a dog a bone This old man came roll-ing home.

3. This old man, he played three,
He played nick-nack on my tree;
Nick-nack, etc.

4. This old man, he played four,
He played nick-nack on my door;
Nick-nack, etc.

5. This old man, he played five,
He played nick-nack on my hive;
Nick-nack,etc.

6. This old man, he played six,
He played nick-nack on my sticks;
Nick-nack, etc.

7. This old man, he played seven,
He played nick-nack down in Devon;
Nick-nack, etc.

8. This old man, he played eight,
He played nick-nack on my gate;
Nick-nack, etc.

9. This old man, he played nine,
He played nick-nack on my line;
Nick-nack, etc.

10. This old man, he played ten,
He played nick-nack on my hen;
Nick-nack, etc.

Polly Wolly Doodle

1. Oh I went down South for to see my Sal, Sing — 'Pol-ly-wol-ly-doo-dle' all the day,
Oh my Sal she am a — mai-den fair, Sing — 'Pol-ly wol-ly doo-dle' all the day,
My — Sal-ly am a — pret-ty gal, Sing 'Pol-ly-wol-ly-doo-dle' all the day.
With — laugh-ing eyes an' — cur-ly hair Sing 'Pol-ly-wol-ly-doo-dle' all the day.
Fare-well! Fare-well! Fare-well!
Fare thee well! Fare thee well! my fair-y fay! Oh, I'm
off to Loui-si-a-nna, for to see my Su-sy An-na, Sing-ing 'Pol-ly wol-ly-doodle' all the day.

3. Oh, a grasshopper sittin' on a railroad track,
Sing 'Polly-wolly-doodle' all the day,
A-pickin' his teef wid a carpet tack,
Sing 'Polly-wolly-doodle' all the day,
Fare thee well, etc.

4. Behind de barn, down on my knees,
Sing 'Polly-wolly-doodle' all the day,
I thought I heard a chicken sneeze,
Sing 'Polly-wolly-doodle' all the day,
Fare thee well, etc.

5. He sneezed so hard wid de whoopin' cough,
Sing 'Polly-wolly-doodle' all the day,
He sneezed his head an' his tail right off,
Sing 'Polly-wolly-doodle' all the day,
Fare thee well, etc.